CW00996682

THE
WIDGET STEPS

ESCALATORS
OF
CAT CARE

by

GAY AND CHRIS ROSE

**With thanks to Ken and Sheelagh - our next door "baby sitters"
and to all cats everywhere.**

The Publishers wish to acknowledge the help and advice given regarding the cartoons in this book by GSP (Global Software Publishing), Meadow Lane, St. Ives, Huntingdon, Cambs, PE17 4LG. Tel: 01480 496666

British Library Cataloguing in Publication Data
Rose, Gay and Chris

The Widget Steps ----- escalators of cat care.
A catalogue record for this book is available from the British Library.

ISBN: 0 9515467 6 7

PUBLISHED BY:
Rosec Publications
135 Church Road
Shoeburyness
Essex SS3 9EZ

PRINTED IN GREAT BRITAIN BY:
Modern Graphic Arts Ltd
52-54 Milton Road
Westcliff on Sea
Essex SSO 7JX

INDEX

INTRODUCTION

The steps were crudely made - by necessity roughly put together in a hurry - but they were a lifeline to the four month old kitten.

With a pair either side of the cat flap she could, at last, join the rest of her family in their outside activities and begin to explore a world that had been denied her.

~~~~~~

There are many good "How To" books about cats and kittens on the market.

This is not a book about famous cats, nor is it a book by famous people. We merely hope that, with humour, and by our own past mistakes, we can help you, the reader, to live happily with your feline friends even if this is your first attempt!

GAY AND CHRIS ROSE

CHAPTER ONE:

FINDING, FEEDING AND SURVIVING THE FIRST WEEK

"At 16 years old she had a fair innings" my husband, Chris, comforted. Neither of us felt any better.

The sad day had arrived. The vet made her last visit. Our poor old moggie, after a short illness, was gently helped through that final cat flap to the sky.

Soon the emptiness of the house began to plunge us into deeper gloom. "I never want to be without a cat again", I wailed.

"This time", we decided, "we'll have two females. We'll let them have one litter each and keep two of <u>their</u> kittens. Double insurance!"

We contacted the Cat's Protection League. We were visited for suitability. "Nobody does this for would-be parents", I muttered darkly. We were told one of their females was 'due' any minute and we could have two of her kittens eight weeks later.

The CPL telephoned when their protégé went into labour. The kittens were **all** black and white. Our favourite colours! A week later they called again to say that all the kittens were male! This was probably just as well since they informed us later that we could not have any kittens unless we signed a form agreeing to have them neutered or spayed at the earliest opportunity!

Kitten-less weeks passed. We telephoned Pet shops who sometimes had calls from private homes when a litter was born. We left our telephone number everywhere!

We found a new Pet shop. The woman proprietor said she'd just sold the last two black and white kittens. The following morning she called back. "You telephoned yesterday", she said, "Well those two I sold - er - well they're back!"

"I'll be there in ten minutes" I said.

I couldn't see them at first because they were in a rabbit hutch and so tiny that the straw half hid them. One was totally black! I looked at the proprietor. "They seem very young", I ventured.

"What can you do?" moaned the woman "people bring them in. I think they're about seven weeks old."

"I don't", I replied. "They've still got blue eyes! They shouldn't leave their mother until they are eight weeks, should they?"

"Well, maybe they were six weeks when I got them. That was a week ago", she retorted.

I didn't want to upset the apple cart too much as I was pretty desperate to get them out of there. The black and white one had the most beautiful markings. The black one was - well - black! And yelling loudly. They both looked extremely scruffy and were standing in their food bowls.

"Um, why, **exactly**, were they sent back?" I asked.

"Well, the people who took them had a little girl. Awful time they had last night. Took her to hospital 'cos she had an asthma attack soon as they showed the kittens to her."

I parted with £20, bought some milk and said I'd be back with my husband before the shop closed that night.

We shot up to a private Cat Care home that we had visited recently so we could buy all the requirements we thought kittens would need - and some they probably didn't!

A very knowledgeable woman ran this place and we were to use her expertise, gained over thirty years of looking after strays, many times in the weeks to come. For the purposes of this book we shall call her Elsa.

Bringing our little 'babies' home in their new cat carrier loaded carefully onto the back seat of the car was a revelation in itself. They cried all the way!

We put them in the shower room along with a scratch post, food bowls, litter trays and 'Igloo' basket. We rushed round like people possessed (which we probably were) preparing milk, kitten food and 'growth' biscuits.

Once all the bowls were topped up we stood back to watch the outcome. Oh dear, not a pretty sight! They zoomed over, promptly stood in one of the bowls and proceeded to behave like a swarm of locusts with the rest of the dishes. The outcome was inevitable. Baby tummies rumbled in unison shortly followed by our furry little friends throwing up all over the carpet.

We immediately got to work cleaning up the mess only to be greeted with explosions from the other end of their anatomies!

The toys we had placed around the room added to the general confusion by becoming various trip hazards for all concerned and the saga ended with two confused little bundles of fluff disappearing into their igloo and gazing at us with sorrowful eyes.

We washed them gently with a flannel dipped in warm water, having read that this represents the rough of their mother's tongue. They began to purr and were promptly sick again.

"I don't think those people who brought them back even **had** a little girl, much less one with asthma", muttered Chris.

We felt totally helpless. That first night we kept getting up to make sure they were still alive. As kittens do, indeed, sleep like the dead, this necessitated going into their room every hour or so!

I telephoned Elsa the following morning.

"For goodness sake don't feed them milk unless diluted with water", she said, "too rich for them, and always leave water down. Can they eat or are they still trying to lap"?

"Eat?!" I cried. "Things just go in one end and straight out the other."

"They're probably much too young to have left their mother", Elsa sighed. "Give them a tiny bit of kitten food and take away what they don't finish. Nothing more for a couple of hours. No cat biscuits unless you moisten them first or they'll likely as not choke on them. Little and often are the watch words."

"I feel so stupid!", I said.

"No you're not, dear. I get **all** sorts. I had a chap call to say his tom was having kittens and I've never forgotten the woman who said her cat kept scratching itself! When I asked her whereabouts it was actually scratching she said 'under the kitchen table'."

We seemed to spend half our time trying to get them to use the litter trays. Chris took to leaving notes for me before he went to work. One morning I came down to read:

"OVERNIGHT: One poo by door, one poo by cat flap, one wee by litter tray, two falls, one submission and a knock out"!

CHAPTER TWO:

NAMES AND NAUGHTY BEHAVIOUR

Bringing up kittens is on a par with bringing up children in that there are various stages to get through before the youth, hopefully, becomes a fairly acceptable adult.

At first Bonnie and Pippa were so tiny that both of them fitted into Chris's hand.

They'd fall asleep on his legs when he sat on the floor.

If we gave them little bits of rolled up paper they would carry these round in their mouths and growl at each other. We'd find them asleep on a radiator towel shelf, or half way up a hanging bathrobe. We'd come home to find they'd moved their igloo from one side of their room to the other.

They'd fight as if demons possessed upstairs and it sounded like thunder! They talked to each other a great deal. Excited little grunts seemed to come from nowhere and then two balls of fur would fly past batting hell out of each other. Five minutes later we would find them fast asleep draped over whatever (or whoever) they'd been playing with. Chris's slippers - when his feet were in them - were a favourite. This could become a little embarrassing if he was sitting on the loo!

Occasionally light smacks were necessary. When accompanied by a loud "No!" the word soon becomes enough. Anyone who has watched a mother cat and it's young (or any other animal apart from the human species) will have seen numerous swats being given.

Litter tray training holds its own qualities and vices. We'd provided a tray for each kitten. It doesn't take a great deal of imagination to work out the horrendous messes this caused. "I'm the King of the Castle" and "Hide and Seek" were two of their favourite games, closely followed by "I can make more mess than you can!" and, naturally, tail chasing in litter trays resulted in the contents being spread from one side of the room to the other "Which one of you is area cleaner for the week?" Chris would demand.

Elsa was consulted. "Put them on their tray immediately they've eaten", she said. "If they make a mess anywhere put a proprietary brand of anti-cat smell down so they don't use that same place again. So long as you clear out any little 'parcels' from the trays, they'll soon start covering it over themselves." We got out some bin liners and a 'scooper'.

We watched them. We soon realised that the occasional low growl from us was enough to send them scooting into their trays whenever they looked like choosing an obscure corner!

We thought the black one was a boy because it had so many lumps and bumps on its bottom! I suggested the name "Hee/She" until we found out what sex it was. Chris wanted to call it "John". As the black and white one made so many peculiar warbling noises in its throat I suggested "Trilla". Chris soon maintained that it didn't really matter what names they were given since they both answered so well to "No!". He also called them babies on 50 mile an hour legs amongst other, less glamorous, things.

It took us at least a fortnight to give them names. Visitors kept asking what we called them.

When we took them to the Vet for their first jabs it was confirmed they were both girls. Eventually the black and white one was called "Pied Piper" which became shortened to "Pippa"

and our little black terror was named "Ebony" which, again, became shortened to "Bonnie".

They were very naughty. The scratch post became unemployed mainly because they found it more fun to hang off all the furniture. When it came to draped towels and the ubiquitous net curtains our sweet little mountain climbers always made it to the top -

wherever the top happened to be! Fascinating squeaks and warbles emitted from their tiny bodies as they dashed up and down the stairs. They would have occasional bouts of jealousy that ended in fisticuffs, quickly followed by sleep - when we discovered they could snore as loudly as humans!

Using the shower room for their 'home' - a cat flap already being in situ - seemed a good notion. However, long before they could use this, they discovered they could reach the loo roll! Once they'd got their claws into the first couple of sheets, what seemed like miles of toilet paper would pile up on the floor! The half door we placed across the entrance seemed a brilliant idea only it didn't take long before they were jumping over it and cuddling up together in some inconspicuous corner of the house.

Pippa, often, was not allowed near us if Bonnie was about. Bonnie was 'top cat'. She began to creep into our study and curl up quietly on Chris's chair whilst I worked. This was fine except that the chair is also black and sometimes she'd get shut in!

Even at this early age we could see both kittens showed many talents. Two that spring readily to mind are knitting and flower arranging. We would come home to find my knitting trailing into every room downstairs and the dried flowers in the lounge neatly arranged all over the floor. The easy answer to the knitting was to hide it. A fragrance holder was placed in front of the dried flowers. Our little terrors hated the smell of this!

Knowing that cats detest eating from dirty bowls a fair amount of washing up was necessary between their meals. They soon told us when they didn't like a particular brand of cat food by trying to cover it up. Cats do not like eating from a dish that is narrower than their whiskers, so a large, flat dish is best.

We learned that whilst they can be 'helpful' when you're cleaning your home they also hate vacuum cleaners. Their hearing is so sensitive that these 'monsters' must sound like pile drivers to them!

CHAPTER THREE:

PUBERTY, TRAINING AND THE TERRIBLE TEENS.

They travelled everywhere in the car with us from a very young age. We would take them along when we visited friends and when we went shopping. By the time we visited relatives in North Wales, some three hundred miles away, they were veterans and afforded much amusement to fellow travellers along the route.

Because of the length of the journey we decided to install their litter tray on the floor in the back of the car. The 'girls' were in their separate baskets on the rear seat. A strangled meow was their way of indicating that they required release so they could visit their 'porta' loo. Bonnie worked this out quite easily. Even at seventy miles per hour her balance was perfect.

What was not so perfect was the result which immediately had us hastily winding down the windows for the next two or three miles! Our car's air freshner couldn't cope.

Pippa was not so easy to please and the idea of crouching over a speeding commode was bang out of order to her. She refused point blank to use the litter tray until we stopped.

We stayed for a week in a cottage near our relatives - who kindly called them "two little power packs" - and although it was hard work with the litter trays and the occasional unravelled loo roll in the utility room where they slept, we believe they enjoyed themselves immensely.

Because of the size of the gardens we took them down to the 'bluebell' woods where they had their first encounter with trees!

Previously they had only encountered their scratch post which went everywhere with us as part of the normal nursery accoutrements.

Coming home we decided to stop for a break and as we were nearing a motorway cafe Chris said "let them out of their baskets - they'll be fine".

As we pulled into the parking area we noticed many amazed looks from other drivers. Pippa was sitting on the top of the passenger seat looking out of the window. Bonnie was perched on Chris's head!

Cat flaps are essential if you don't wish to keep your cat in forever - with all the attendant problems this can bring. It amused us to read that Isaac Newton, a great cat lover, cut a small opening in a barn door so that his female cat could freely come and go. When kittens arrived he cut a smaller hole next to the original.

If our kittens saw rain outside their cat flap they tended to be puzzled by the fact that when they tried another outlet, such as the kitchen door, it was also raining out there!

By propping the cat flap open with a small piece of wood to begin with we found they soon got the right idea. We put their litter tray just outside for the first couple of days then gradually moved it a little further away until the litter could be tipped onto the garden earth. The kittens followed this natural progression.

Once they had grown a little we put small harnesses on them and let them get used to these before attaching leads each time we took them into the garden. They were terrified of everything in sight at first and we often ended up in complete disarray with their leads wrapped round our legs.

We would find them halfway up our flowering cherry - stuck fast and yelling loudly. For some unknown reason kittens do not understand that they have to turn round once they have climbed something and attempt a backward slither!

Bonnie, the placid, liked to lie in the laundry basket, empty or not, until the day she turned it over on herself and all we could see was a slowly moving yellow cage followed - and being batted by - Pippa.

Pippa, the restless, had a habit (which she has to this day) of jumping onto our laps, kneading like mad for a couple of seconds, giving a little trill and leaping off again.

Both of them loved to jump on moving toes underneath the bed covers. They would then proceed to shake themselves and fall off. It is not polite to laugh at cats - they do not like it. Naturally enough they would end up tearing down the stairs in a huff!

CHAPTER FOUR:

WORMS, FLEAS ....

"Elsa", we asked, "why is Pippa dragging her bottom along the floor?"

"Worms!" she said succinctly. We obtained a milky substance from the Vet that we introduced into their mouths by way of a baby feeder. They hated it. It worked.

There are many good treatments available for fleas and worms, for both kittens and cats. Some instructions can make highly amusing reading.

Idly leafing through some pamphlets on the latest flea spray we read: "Stand cat on piece of paper and rub its fur up the wrong way before spraying". There are various things cats do not like. One of them is standing still. Need we say more?

A lovely story was printed some time ago in the Reader's Digest. This involved some poor chap who had to try and get several pills down its feline friend's throat. Every time he tried he got bitten and scratched. One day, in the usual struggle, he dropped both tablet and cat. The cat looked at him, looked at the pill on the floor, sniffed it - and ate it!

We can only surmise this was Synulox - an antibiotic which cats actually love. What a blessing modern veterinary medicines are.

One of the best preparations currently on the market is Frontline. This can be used either as a spray or a 'spot on'. Cats, in particular, tend to be more sensitive to some of the other preparations.

Fur balls are another bane for cats. Try mixing 5ml of liquid paraffin into their food or, alternatively, your vet will probably prescribe "Catalax" which most cats like the taste of.

Young cats become extremely interested in anything which is smaller than they are, especially if it moves. Sodium bicarbonate in a little warm water is useful for the high probability of bites and stings.

.... AND FRIGHTS IN THE NIGHT

Once kittens have received all their jabs they can be shown the great outdoors. Eventually the terrors of the litter tray can be exchanged for things that are usually hauled in by them at night. This may be their way of saying "thank you" but unfortunately can also lead to the odd panic attack for their doting owners.

When our two began bringing in leaves and twigs, or snickering and waggling their bottoms at flies we ignored them, thinking this would have the same effect as the method used on a child who suddenly comes home with a swear word! It doesn't work with cats.

We have a pond with Koi Carp. Asking for trouble we guess. Ponds tend to have a fair quantity of toads and frogs in their vicinity.

Cats soon learn to keep well away from toads since these creatures give off a nasty smell and taste revolting if the cat bites hard enough. The smell the toad gives off when it senses danger is usually more than enough. Frogs are another matter!

"Bonnie tried to come through the cat flap carrying what looked like a bag of dirty washing", Chris said, "but we had a show down at the flap door and she shot away again."

We had a blackbird who visited for raisins every morning during the breeding season. The kittens would snicker like billio and rush out - not quite knowing why - then pretend to catch flies instead. This particular blackbird even found its way into our lounge!

Bells on collars are a must. Mind you, when they fall asleep on the end of the bed they usually end up having a fight and there is generally enough bell ringing to wake the dead. This can be very annoying at 5 am in the morning!

We use fluorescent collars on our bunch. A small name and telephone number tag, along with the bell, is useful. At least with the bells **we** know where they are!

Bonnie was first over the neighbouring fences and she had a penchant for moths! We would hear her bell outside on the front pavement as she chased them and would have to get up and call her in.

Just before he left for work one morning Chris saw her right at the top of a very large fir tree next door. No problem really except that he had to get her down again since she was stuck!

Once they both found their way from the back of the house to the front we would clap our hands and shoo them back again, especially if a car passed. They seemed to get the message although occasionally when we returned from a walk we would see them both trotting up the street to meet us.

CHAPTER FIVE:

UNINVITED GUESTS ....

Young cats get very excited by things

and then bore easily!

"Who owns this frog"? Chris would yell.

We remain constantly amazed at how two cats can get through one cat flap at the same time!

We'd be talking on the telephone that stood on the table in the hall and hear 'reddit' coming from somewhere near. My usual note to Chris was, "There's a frog somewhere in the house!"

Most nights in summer would see cats, frogs and toads cavorting on the lawn together. It was not unusual to go downstairs in the night and step on something squishy!

Chris left a note. "Left Pippa happily playing with her toys. Bonnie was eating worms."

We resorted to shutting all the doors to the main rooms. Returning home from shopping one day, and before going out again, I wrote a note for Chris who had obviously been home that lunchtime.

"You left the study light on and the door wide open".

When I returned **his** note read "and you left the back door open and a cat locked in the kitchen!"

Beds are for hiding behind. Little heads suddenly pop up just as you are falling asleep thinking you've shut them out for the night.

Pippa does not like water from the tap. Its pool or rain water - nothing else! She will go to extraordinary lengths to get her own way. We have watched her playing with the ice on the bird bath, picking at it with her claws and flipping the ice out onto the ground so she can have a drink!

We once found her on top of the waterfall in the middle of our pool. How she jumped that distance without falling in will never be known.

We have even seen her walking across the ice that blankets the pool netting on a wintry night.

One of Chris's notes read:

"Well you missed a classic this morning! CURTAIN OPENS: 07.30

Pippa shoots to the side of the pool hoping to catch a passing 'reddit'. Bonnie meantime creeps up behind the ever hopeful frog catcher and belts her one on the backside. Pippa shoots about a yard in the air, does a cracking somersault and lands in the pond on the lily pads.

She then proceeds to 'doggy' paddle right across to the other side of the pool, and, as if with a rocket up her rear end, disappears into the blue yonder!"

CHAPTER SIX:

PREGNANCY AND PALPITATIONS

It probably goes without saying that the palpitations are generally yours!

We did not want Bonnie and Pippa to have their kittens while they were too young and discussed this with the Vet. There is an injection available that puts off the urge for up to six months but, strangely enough, they never needed it. Perhaps being semi long hairs had something to do with it. They were nine months old before they became interested in the opposite sex!

Both of them were very sly about their mating. We didn't even know they had come into season as the usual signs of 'calling' and rolling over were absent and as they are normally very loving anyway, we didn't notice any special spurts of friendliness.

'Cat flap opportunists', as one writer so cleverly put it, seemed to suddenly appear. We wondered what on earth the new kittens would be like since, if a female mates with more than one male each kitten will pick up different characteristics and colours from each 'father'.

It was New Year's Eve when we noticed a large ginger tom lurking outside the cat flap. Neither of our girls seemed too bothered. However on New Year's Day this male was back again together with four more! Chris decided to act the doting Dad and locked the cat flap to keep them out.

Neither Pippa nor Bonnie were at all enamoured with this idea, especially as they were suddenly presented with a litter tray again. They spent half the night fighting each other and 'picking' at the carpets thus keeping us awake until we gave in!

During the next few days we watched various fisticuffs going on between Bonnie, Pippa and the various toms. Sometimes all we could see were various parts of the garden on the move as they semi fought, semi played with their new friends! If there was only one tom around this usually resulted in him zooming off at a rate of knots, being unable to choose between them.

All went very quiet for a couple of days and then Bonnie came in with a bloody ear and Pippa started dashing around the house trying to kill her beanbag, the carpet and anything else in sight. Chris found 'someone' had pulled up the mat in their room and done a whoopsie underneath!

At last we came home one evening to see what can only be described as a tableau of cats all doing what comes naturally. We rather liked one of the handsome young tabbies and the black and white male but couldn't see what our girls saw in the tatty old ginger tom!

Most of the mating was done on our next door neighbour's rockery. The daughter of the house apparently came home one night and went indoors with a very indignant look on her face.

"I don't know what that black and white tom was doing to Bonnie but it was biting her neck and obviously hurting her so I kicked it off!"

"You'd never think she was 21 years old would you?", laughed her mother when relating the story.

We got so used to losing sight of them all night that we got in the habit of thinking they were out when they weren't. One morning we found Pippa had been shut in the lounge and the next day noticed Bonnie's delicate black paw whizzing back and forth under the garage door!

By mid February a visit to the Vet confirmed that both of them were well and truly pregnant.

Now the waiting game began until the middle of March.

The girls were healthy, glossy and just as madcap as ever.

Their latest trick was to capture small pre-formed pieces of polystyrene packing - usually floating around in the breeze somewhere. Today's manufacturers have a lot to answer for! Wonder how they'd feel if they had to clean up hundreds of minute balls of the stuff from their own carpets!

CHAPTER SEVEN:

MOTHERHOOD AND MAYHEM:

Bonnie went into labour at 9.30 PM on March 7th, 1995. She had a very determined look on her face - almost a pursing of the lips - as she pushed. All we could see from her rear was a tiny black tail and hind legs. Oh great - a **breech** birth!

"They're all going to be black, like her", Chris moaned.

At 11.50 PM her first son came into the world. Wow - that first cry! We suddenly knew how grandparents felt!

Immediately she was pulling at the afterbirth which covered the tiny thing. Then she ate it. We'd heard about this and how essential it is for the first feeds but it is not for the faint hearted!

As the kitten's fur dried we realised it was pure tabby.

Her second tabby was born one hour later and the birth only took five minutes. The third, and last, was at 3 AM by which time Chris had gone to bed and I was drooping on my 'watch stool'.

Once all were safely delivered, well washed down by their mother and fed we all managed a few hours sleep. About 8 AM Bonnie carried her first born upstairs. She held him awkwardly in her mouth, somewhere between his neck and the middle of his back, which is probably why he was squawking so loudly!

"I don't think so dear," Chris said quietly to her, "I really don't think the landing should become a nursery for the troops, sweetie, do you?" Obligingly she took her son back to the others.

A first litter must seem as scary to a cat as a first baby to a human mother. A new mother cat will often move it's kittens if it feels they are threatened in any way, or if they think there is something wrong with one of them. Pippa, still heavily pregnant, may have worried Bonnie somewhat.

The following morning we could not find Bonnie or her kittens. Eventually we realised she had taken them all into the shower cubicle with her! A call to Elsa ascertained that mother cats quite often 'wander' after giving birth and to keep an eye on them all.

Bonnie was out in the garden with me a few days later. She decided to dig a hole near to where I was deadheading some flowers. The most appalling smell drifted over to me followed by a loud fart! The poor girl had diarrhoea. This is fairly normal as the stomach settles. I had made the mistake of feeding her, just once, with some milk supplement and it had definitely not agreed with her!

Another call to Elsa evoked the response that the best thing to do was leave her without food for 24 hours and only give her water. Sure enough she was fine.

Pippa was late! We waited whilst she lay about in heavy anticipation, drooling over Bonnie's kittens when allowed and generally being totally fed up. She needed many cuddles!

She did not go into labour until six days later. That Sunday afternoon she moved about constantly from room to room. She then insisted on lying with Bonnie's kittens and, luckily, Bonnie didn't seem to mind.

Eventually her first contractions began but she kept trying to get out of the box we had put her in and sit in the litter tray. We gave her little sips of water from our fingers because she was pretty scared and panting a great deal.

She took so long heaving with the first one that we thought about calling the Vet.

"It's been two hours and it's her first litter", we worried.

Eventually - around midnight - she produced a black, white and tabby kitten.

We wondered why Bonnie kept grunting in her throat and trying to get into the shower cubicle where Pippa had decided to give birth to the rest of her babies. We kept shoving her away. Pippa was doing everything correctly but, unfortunately, went almost straight into delivery of the next kitten. We let Bonnie in with her.

It totally amazed us when we realised that Bonnie was stripping the afterbirth and eating it before licking down Pippa's second kitten. It was just as well because Pippa seemed extremely weak. Bonnie also kept moving her own kittens all over the place so the area was like Waterloo Station!

Pippa's third, which appeared to be black and white striped but, once dry, ended up tortoiseshell with white paws, was born at 12.45 AM.

Bonnie scurried between Pippa and her own kittens. However, there was an enormous load of farting going on in the shower cubicle (accompanied by giggles from us) and she gave up at 2 AM when Pippa delivered her fourth and last. This little one appeared to be black, white and tortoiseshell with a totally black head and ginger ears!

She also seemed to have something wrong with her back legs.

The following morning we found Pippa feeding two of Bonnie's kittens so we changed them all round again and gave their boxes a good clean out. A call to Elsa again. Although it is quite natural for another female cat to **occasionally** feed another cat's kitten, we were very luck to have two who seemed to shared so naturally!

It came to the crunch when, after a couple of days, it became apparent that Pippa could only be bothered to feed one or two and Bonnie was taking the brunt. Bonnie was obviously not too happy with the situation and kept moving the kittens.

We kept putting Pippa's kittens back in with her until she settled with them and began to feed them properly. This didn't last very long however and she showed a definite tendency to be quite happy with the first two born to her but not at all bothered about the last two - especially the very last with her funny little, splayed out, hind legs.

We even tried separating the families into different rooms but this only caused consternation between the mothers and eventually - once we had shut the shower cubicle door and put their two large baskets outside - they all appeared to settle down. For that first week, however, there was constant movement from one area of the house to another.

We would find one
family behind
our bed

and the others under the
telephone table!

30

CHAPTER EIGHT:

KITTEN INVASION.

We got in a dreadful muddle with them all. Someone who saw the first photographs said they'd make a lovely jigsaw.

What continued to amaze and amuse us was the way they would feed each other's babies. Mind you, a great deal of the time the only sight we had of Pippa was her back legs disappearing through the cat flap as she decided to take a lengthy stroll in the garden. Often she looked as if she was contemplating getting her hair permed!

We continued to plonk her kittens on her because she tended to ignore them. We tried to tell poor Bonnie that seven into six doesn't go! She was the perfect little mother whilst Pippa, we're afraid, was not cut out for it.

Elsa told us it's the luck of the draw. Some cats are good mothers and some are not - a little like humans really.

When Pippa's 'runt' was three weeks old I asked Chris to take her to the Vet since her back legs were still splayed out and she appeared weak and very small. We were told that she was not in pain and although her hind legs would never be completely straight she would eventually walk fairly normally and grow up to be just as active as the others. Rickets was the problem and we were advised to try and hand feed her.

We experienced sheer frustration. It may look easy in pictures in books but hand feeding can be mind boggling! There you are, trying to get nourishment into an animal no bigger than your fist and all it does is cry piteously and spill the milk all over itself and you! Bonnie would usually give us a commiserating look and take over!

Obviously there were altercations. We would hear the mothers fighting and go down to find the little one shrieking with a very wet neck and only Bonnie with her. In the animal kingdom we suppose she represented something "not quite right" and was being rejected.

At first we nicknamed her "Bouncy" because she used to make her way along by using her front legs and dragging her hind legs behind her, rather than jumping about like the others.

We had to go away when they were four weeks and three weeks old respectively but they were quite happy all together in the cattery. Bonnie, bless her, had trained her kittens to use the litter tray. "Bouncy" was walking - very slowly and very carefully to be sure, but walking! Sadly this hadn't appeared to improve the relationship between herself and her mother.

Bonnie seemed to sense this and would often move the little thing into another room. Every time she did this Pippa would come after her, take it away, carry it somewhere else and leave it there! We were forever putting this tiny scrap in with her mother yet, when we looked to see if she was feeding her, we would find that, again, Pippa was feeding the rest while "Bouncy" sat despondently outside the basket!

It seemed that Pippa was always trying to either kill her last born or love her to death and it was an extremely trying time for us all.

Bonnie was forever taking care of her "niece", constantly licking and feeding her. Without Bonnie we do not think she would have survived.

We named her Widget!

Suddenly the kittens were everywhere. Bonnie's eldest - obviously the largest and most daring - found his way upstairs when he was only five weeks old. In another week he was outside by the coal bunker having followed one of the mothers straight out through the still open cat flap!

Worming seven kittens each day for three days is no joke especially when you have to weigh them all first to make sure they are getting the right dosage!

Widget began to use the litter tray and to take small bits of food from our fingers.

We began to have fun with them. Kittens love anything that crackles. Small bits of paper wadded up in a ball or scraps of selotape are favourites. One kitten got a piece of selotape stuck to its tail and the others watched with dizzy eyes as it went round and round in a circle like a spinning Catherine wheel.

Eventually all the kittens were using the litter trays but occasionally there would still be the odd accident.

Bonnie, the watcher, 'called' us one night. This was so unusual that we had to investigate. We went down to find that one of the kittens had left a mess in the middle of their food!

"Who did that!?", I would ask on seeing something obnoxious left in a corner.

"How do I know?" came Chris's mournful reply. "No-one left a signature on it!"

CHAPTER NINE:

TO KEEP OR NOT TO KEEP.

We wanted to keep them all but it was impossible. We decided on Widget, because she was so little, so loving and such a laughter maker.

Bonnie's eldest was our other choice because he'd managed to jump over the half door when he was eight weeks old and was the type of kitten who, given a pink fluffy mouse on a bungy attached to a large, flat base would somehow manage to drag the whole thing from one room to another and end up looking, from the resultant mouthfuls of fur, as if he had just shaved! We named him Phoenix.

By the time Pippa and Bonnie were due to be spayed three of the kittens had found new homes. We had arranged for one of them to go the night before the girls went in to have their operations. Two more were due to leave on the day. We checked with the Vet that this would be ok and were told they didn't think there would be a problem in the girls arriving home to find some of their brood no longer there.

Chris thought it would be a good idea to put a collar and bell on the first kitten to leave. We did this the night before so we could pick it out easily in the morning. The kitten didn't mind the collar and bell in the least - what it did mind was all the other kittens thinking it was a new toy! They chased it all round the room with glee!

We felt very sad when we took this funny little chap to his new home. At first, quite naturally - he hid behind one of the cabinets in his new parents' kitchen. Eventually he decided to explore and ended up in their dog's basket which pleased everyone but the dog! They were soon, however, to become the best of friends not only sleeping in the same bed but rambling everywhere together.

When we returned we found that Phoenix had got out again and was yelling behind the coal bunker and Pippa had taken two of her kittens and hidden them behind our bed!

The next day bought the departure of two more kittens combined with the 'ops for Pippa and Bonnie.

Both of them were fairly groggy when we bought them home in the evening and as we didn't want them inadvertently treading on their youngsters whilst still half asleep, we shut them away from the kittens for the night. I was woken by Bonnie's purr and her paws kneading my stomach - bless her.

She seemed quite pleased the next morning to be allowed back with her babies and continued to feed them as if nothing had happened. We were a little concerned that the kittens might try and play with her stitches but she was very careful to lie on that side so they couldn't.

Pippa eventually woke up and decided she ought to give her own babies a cursory lick and a half hearted "hello". She then decided to go out and was, yet again, followed by Phoenix. He merely shot out underneath her whilst she was still halfway through the flap. Another rescue operation had to be made!

There remained two kittens to find homes for. We made out C.V.'s!

MY C.V.!!

Hallo! I am your new kitten. I am not sure, yet, whether I am a girl or a boy. I do not have a name because my Mummy thought you would like to call me something yourself - as long as it's not rude!

I was born in the early hours of Wednesday, 8th March 1995 and my mother's name is Bonnie. She is a black cat and very affectionate and sweet natured.

My first injection against those nasty illnesses that cats can get should be on 10th May. I don't expect I shall like it very much. Anyway - I have to have some more three weeks later! Oh yes - I was given some nasty stuff called "Panacur Wormer" on the 26th, 27th and 28th April. My grandparents got this from someone called a "Vet" who also gave them a sort of measured bottle to put it in because I am so tiny. I shall need some more on 18th May and then every three weeks after that.

In case I do something I shouldn't in my new home perhaps I should tell you that I have also got used to something called "CATSAN" which is a white litter.

*I have grown up on Hill's Science "Growth" biscuits (which are very good for me) and Felix Original tinned food. Little and often please. I like water but not milk or any milk supplement. My tastes **may** change. I'd like some toys to play with - especially as I will miss my mummy and my brothers and sisters very much for a little while.*

PS. My grandparents say that if I am a girl and you don't want me to have any kittens I should visit the "Vet" when I am about six months old. I shouldn't have any kittens until I am about a year old anyway, so if you do want me to have some there is an "injection" from the "Vet" that lasts until I'm grown up enough!

*If I am a boy then I don't have to visit a "Vet" until I am about nine months old. Actually, if I **am** a boy, I don't have to go at all but it would be kinder because then I wouldn't get into any fights.*

I hope we have lots of fun together over the years and that you will always tell my grandparents how I am getting on because they worry a bit!

Lots of love, xxxx

One more was homed and there remained just one of Bonnie's little girls. She had sad eyes - almost as if she was saying "why can't I stay here?!"

It was not long, however, before a family of six came round, en masse, immediately fell in love with her and took her home there and then, having already sorted out jabs at vets, etc. They were kind enough to call that evening to say that she had settled down really well.

So - the "famous five" found new homes. Chris let out a sigh of relief and said, "There's not going to be quite so much of a problem as far as crowd control is concerned"!

CHAPTER TEN:

GROWING PAINS.

We know of one couple who called their two kittens "Dyne" and "Mite", otherwise known as the demolition squad! Two of our kittens went to couples who kept us well abreast of their antics and even sent us a couple of letters - as if from the kittens themselves.

"There is a big cat here who doesn't seem very keen on me. Mummy says she'll be alright once I know my place. She says I'm going to grow up to be a "Holy Terror", whatever that is. She's got something called a 'Duvet' which is great fun. Both of us cats often purr on it and Mummy says she supposes purring in stereo will at least drown Daddy's snoring. My new name is "Jessica". My new Daddy says I'll probably be called 'that bloody cat' most of the time!"

"Dear Granny and Grandpa

I'm in deep trouble.

I got bored one night and had a session round the bed, up the headboard and up the light pull. This was at 4 AM which seemed quite a reasonable time to me but as I also climbed the wallpaper to a height of three feet I am now banished to the kitchen.

My big sister sometimes lets me play with her but she seems to have a bit of a short fuse and I often get my ears boxed.

I'm twice as big now as when I left you. Mummy says if I reach adulthood it will be a miracle!"

You can feel pretty embarrassed at times!

Chris kept asking our two which part of "No" they didn't understand!

By twelve weeks, although they still occasionally fed from their mothers, they were getting along fine with bulk food. They grew in fits and starts - Phoenix at an alarming rate! He had his first jab the same day that the girls had their stitches out. Unfortunately poor Widget had to wait another week for her first injection and then it was Phoenix's turn for his second lot and then Widget again! Phew! We always took them both in, as company for each other, even if one wasn't being dealt with that day.

Of course, Pheonix was racing around outside as soon as both his jabs had been given. He was not exactly a friendly kitten to start with. He was bold and an 'early starter' but he was also nervy, probably because we had not given him enough attention earlier in his life because of the time needed to look after all the others. He also had his mother, aunt and cousin to play with so did not rely on us as they had. It took weeks of gradual petting to get him to start trusting us enough for a cuddle.

He got rather confused in those early days because if he brought in a dead mouse we told him he was a good boy. Birds or frogs were entirely another matter! We found a young starling hiding on top of a wardrobe upstairs and not long after another in the kitchen. Rescue operations abounded.

With four young cats on the prowl there were far more frogs roaming round the house. We could usually tell when there was one lurking somewhere since all four cats would sit and look fixedly at the same spot!

I found a frog behind their litter tray- being studiously ignored by them all - and another in the dining room that had obviously been sneaked in whilst Chris was having his breakfast and before he left for work shutting the dining room door behind him.

One morning we opened their door to find their litter all over the floor. One frog sat in the middle of this and another was underneath the radiator. Bonnie, Phoenix and Pippa took one look at us and shot out of the cat flap. Widget just looked tired! She had not been involved because she was still house bound. Shortly after I had despatched one frog back to the pond the three cats came back in. I was picking up the frog underneath the radiator which I thought was dead. It gave a giant leap, I gave a giant scream and three cats shot out again!

A frog, if left too long indoors will dry out and die. We tried leaving a couple of corpses on their feeding bowls (feeding Widget separately) and even went so far as to hang two dead ones outside the cat flap, but we don't think they ever really got the message!

Widget would retire upstairs and fall asleep on our bed. She was still so tiny! She was often left alone. She did not have enough strength in her back legs to stand on them and push open the cat flap. Even though we would let her out via the kitchen door so she could enjoy the garden, she still had to rely far too much on us.

We would let her back in again and she would moan and mooch around the house. Thus the "Widget Steps" were born!

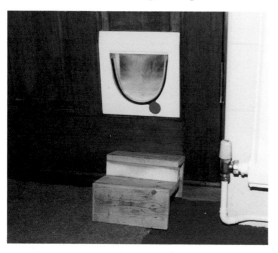 

The steps that Chris built for Widget were necessary if she was not to be left behind in the first few weeks of the others' great outdoor adventures. She was pathetically grateful once these were in situ.

Very soon she was in and out like a miniature jack in the box - rushing back with great joy to tell us she had just killed two leaves! She had found a measure of independence but was still left behind once the others had jumped over the neighbouring fences.

It was not until she was five months old that she finally made the top of the birdbath - this being all of one foot high! She spent ages scooping the water out all over the patio, until she slipped off!

We bought them Ping-Pong balls with bells inside which charmed them immensely - along with their mothers!

Finding my wool - yet again - all over the house, I got really fed up with them and, shutting them in the lounge I smacked the edge of the sofa with a fly swatter and shouted "No!". Phoenix tried to jump up the closed door and Widget shot behind the sofa.

We found that despite being twice the size of Widget her cousin was extremely gentle with her. We worried sometimes when playtime got a bit rough in case he was getting too mature and tried it on with her before it was time to have them 'fixed'!

We would find them asleep in the laundry basket together (clothes in or not!) or cuddled together on top of their chair in the lounge.

In the summer of that year we decided, a bit late in the day because all the kittens had left or grown up, to have lino put down in their room. There was a problem in that the floor underneath the carpet needed screeding and so all the cats had to spend a couple of nights in the cattery whilst this was laid down and allowed to set.

Before they went in Pippa was acting very oddly - being a 'scaredy-cat'! She kept shooting in from the garden yet every time we looked around we could see nothing. Once they were in the cattery we closed the cat flap against other cats and retired to bed.

About 2 AM we were woken by a terrible racket! Someone, or something, was banging and crashing at the cat flap. We shot down there to find the whole flap - even the surround - torn from its hinges and laying on the floor inside the room. There had been no animal noises at all. Something with terrific strength had obviously tried to get in. To this day we have no idea of what it could have been, nor why! We had to buy another cat flap and fit it before we could get our family home!

Bell ringing became quite a past-time in our house. Or rather listening to it! Bonnie would shake her bells twice. Pippa was fairly obvious because she wore three. Phoenix would always give one shake of his head and Widget would go on forever and yell as well! Bells work though. Pippa was once without hers for three days having 'lost' them somehow, and she caught as many birds.

Bonnie and Widget were still catching worms which at last prompted us to shut them in for the night by leaving just the "in" part of the flap working. Only we also caught a new cat to the neighbourhood who'd come in search of food! My goodness, did he dash round that room before we could get the 'out' catch on. We didn't think he'd try again and we were right!

Those strange clockwork balls attached to furry ferret toys are fun. Our cats just stare as the thing whizzes round and round. They won't go near until it stops. Then they kill it like mad!

CHAPTER ELEVEN:

THE UNKINDEST CUT.

It is worth remembering that no self respecting cat will shove its paw in the air to volunteer a visit to the vet, either to have things propelled down its throat or popped up its rear!

Since cats don't know the difference between a visit to the vet and other outings as both involve "cat carriages", it is wise to remind oneself that whatever method and cat box is used this will normally become a full scale exercise.

There are differing opinions in the cat world about the easiest way to put cats into the new 'front loading' cat carriers! Some say backing them in is best. Chris says that he, personally, has never seen a cat walk backwards! He states that although they start the exercise with four legs it is totally amazing how your friendly domestic moggie soon shows its split personality and turns into a furry octopus!

No matter how many legs you think are pinned against their sides, mysteriously (and usually painfully) another leg seems to grow from nowhere! Chris feels that fast forward is best, even if you do get the occasional bat wing appearing to halt the procedure. It has been known for him to tip the basket on end and drop the cat backwards into it but only when he's had enough!

Expense is one thing to take well into account before you have any animal. However to know that your new addition to the family has been injected and rendered safe from the "nasties" is well worth it.

Three major illnesses are still responsible for the death of most cats. The first and second visit that your kitten makes to a Vet are extremely important and cannot be recommended enough. Normally the first visit should be when they are eight weeks old and the booster three weeks after that. At eight weeks a kitten is not getting the antibodies from its mother any more even though she may still be feeding it.

If you don't intend to let your female cat have kittens then it is usually necessary to have her spayed at around five months of age. The male cat can be left until around eight or nine months.

When we thought it was time for Widget and Phoenix to be 'fixed' we were advised by the Vet to wait until Widget was six months old as, being small and long haired, it wasn't thought she would be at risk - even from her rather ardent young cousin! We worried that Phoenix's boisterous nature would overpower Widget whilst she was recovering so we had both operated on at the same time and at least they were company for each other.

Since we'd had problems trying to spray them for fleas and they had not taken kindly to flea wipes either, they were given a thorough dosing whilst still out for the count. Normally veterinary practices will spray your cat for you free of charge but please remember to leave something in the charity box. Widget was also X-rayed as she was still very small. She needed calcium to build up her bones. She loved the pills and we had to be careful that she got to them before the others beat her to it!

In July 1996 Pippa appeared with what looked like blood on her coat but was gone again so quickly that we didn't have time to see what was wrong.

She disappeared almost completely for two days but, seemingly to save our sanity, put in a brief appearance halfway up the garden for a couple of minutes each night. She would give each cat a cursory lick and be gone again.

All our neighbours were alerted and at 7 AM on the third day our friends next door telephoned to say they'd seen her in their garden, called her and she'd come into their house! We thanked God that all our cats are so fond of our neighbours! We carted her off to the Vet where it was necessary for her to have eight stitches.

A huge collar had been 'clipped' round her neck - obviously to stop the unfortunate patient trying to remove the sutures. Chris got the giggles. "Oh my, a black and white moving lampshade", he whispered, "Or a French Nun!" When Pippa woke up properly she could not eat or drink with this collar on. Although she tried she kept bumping into things and getting confused. We took it off once we realised that she would not gnaw at her stitches.

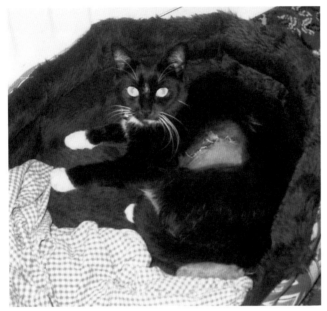

We kept her away from the others (with little visits allowed for a few minutes each day) and she lived in the dining room and kitchen for about a week! Then she got an abscess and had to have four more stitches!

Our first thoughts, dreadful as it seems, were that she had been shot at with an air rifle but the Vet told us that somehow she'd caught herself on some old wire somewhere. Being long haired definitely hadn't helped her!

Chris came up one morning and said "you're quite right, I'd never make a Vet!" and then watched in amazement as I fed Pippa her antibiotic tablet. The trick was to give it to her when the others were around so she would eat it before they could!

She got extremely bored being shut in the kitchen all the time. Sometimes she hid to frighten us again! Especially in the small gap between two kitchen units that housed the towel rail!

Bonnie took to sitting in our bath which we, in turn, took to mean she wanted some attention. Loads of cuddles were required.

When we took Pippa in to have her final stitches out we also took Phoenix to have his ears examined. Even the vet was trying not to laugh! We don't know who was more embarrassed - us or poor Phoenix. There sat this huge cat emitting what can only be described as a high pitched squeak. "Obviously he was neutered properly!" we said. Since then he only gives us the silent meow!

Widget is one of those cats that will take on any task that the others would cock a snook at. The one that really fascinates us is the, "I'm in vacuum mode!" In layman's terms this translates as "whatever it is on the floor I'll eat it and be damned to the consequences"! The consequences, more often than not, are little puddles everywhere as she promptly empties the 'vacuum bag'!

She came in one morning and was promptly sick. This went on for a couple of days so it was off to the vet again. She had a temperature so they kept her in. We were told that she may have to have a light injection and a search of her throat and stomach.

Maybe she would even need a full anaesthetic to be X-rayed since cats do **not** sit still for these! Chris told her to "be inexpensive" and she was. A fur ball had been the problem.

We had already decided it was time for a new scratch post for them all and, as a treat for them after all the 'hoo-ha' we finally bought one!

Catteries are another kind of 'cut'. Many people seem to think it is cruel to leave a cat cooped up for a couple of weeks. However, it is even more cruel to leave them at home without your company for more than a few days.

We found an excellent cattery that came highly recommended from out Vet and all the cats are so happy there that they think it a frightful bore when it is time to come home.

Nowadays the cattery collects and delivers them. However, one of the 'hilights?' of this is when the cattery owner says "oh look they seem to have had an upset" and it is only on further inspection that you realise - with dismay - that you have been presented with the full 'Monty'! Could someone invent a dirt box for cat baskets?

Once home they usually shoot all over the house and then disappear for a few hours into the garden before coming in to settle down. Widget, especially, needs much exercise as she takes ages to 'unscrunch'!

You may have, as we do, the kindest neighbours who adore your cats but, mostly, it is not fair to ask them to accept responsibility for too long. If you only have one cat this may work out, but our four can be quite a handful! Believe it or not cats look for their owners almost as much as dogs do and, therefore, tend to roam.

We tried it once, for longer than a few days, over the Christmas period. Arriving home we were greeted with the exit of four very disgruntled moggies through the cat flap. During the unpacking Chris noticed that some of the landing carpet had been 'taken up'.

I soon realised that for some unknown reason there didn't appear to be any paper on the loo roll holder in their room. Then we found our neighbours' poem - as if 'written' by the cats!

"Welcome back home, we hope you've had a good time
We've all been good, like you told us we should
and everything here has been fine.
We got a bit bored and wanted some fun
and thought we'd start on the mat
but her from next door came in and proclaimed
"Oh no! You mustn't do that!"

Top of the stairs seemed a good place to go
To exercise our claws
But again she came in, gasped in dismay
And threatened to smack all our paws!
We then discovered some feathers
Enough for us all
And had a good game up and down in the hall

The best was the snow as it came in profusion
Causing chaos, havoc and much confusion
But for us it's been great to play out of doors
And not worry about **her** rules when sporting on floors!"

It took a few days for them to stop playing havoc with our loo rolls and it was a couple of weeks before we thought the landing carpets would survive.

However Phoenix decided, again, to remove the carpet. Only this time Chris proclaimed that he was "in charge" and made the point very, very clearly that the carpet was staying where it was! Perhaps the problem began when he tried to extricate Phoenix by the scruff of his neck and take him downstairs. Chris came second. The ambulance man said that apart from the blood and the lumps on his hands and arms he didn't need any stitches but maybe a Tetanus shot would be a good idea!

CHAPTER TWELVE:

THE GARDENING CLUB.

This can be a real problem - especially if you love your garden as much as we do!

We had two new rockeries put in the front garden. Chris came bursting in one evening and pointed an accusing finger at Pippa. "Percy Thrower has been at it again!" he fumed.

We tried all the normal remedies. Nothing worked. Holes were everywhere and even our neighbours began to look a bit harassed once the kittens were old enough to 'visit'!

We discovered what must be a very old idea when we went North to see our son one weekend. We asked what the white chips were all over their neighbour's garden. Firelighters! Cut them up into small pieces and sprinkle round your plants. Cats won't go near them for at least a fortnight as they hate the smell.

Of course if it rains these don't last so long and we ended up using an expensive but effective method whenever planting new shrubs. Fine netting, net pegs and bark chips are required. Whenever you plant, surround the new growth with netting held in place by the pegs and cover the lot with bark. We found that the cats only tried to dig once and then left the area well alone.

Pippa loves it when we do the gardening, not to mention helping us feed the fish. She loves the fish pellets!

Bonnie decided to get under the pond net one morning and couldn't get out again. Phoenix and Widget thought this was a great game and kept smacking her every time she tried. She slid, she got her back feet wet, she was thoroughly fed up!

If you happen to have a pond in your own garden, and have cats, be careful what you introduce. I was not happy when someone offered us two small Sturgeons and then told us they feed on their backs. Frogs get too near the surface as well! Widget brought one of the Sturgeon into their room on the first night and the next day we found a fish head by the garage. She also brought a frog in and was so pleased with herself that she woke us all up!

She went missing one day. As this was before she began to clamber over fences I could not understand why she was not in the garden. It was also raining.   The other three were jumping backwards and forwards into the garden that backs onto ours! Eventually I heard a faint squealing.

Widget had made it to the top of the fence and fallen off on the wrong side! I tried putting various things over in the hope that she would climb them - without success. She shot off somewhere. I resorted to going round the long way to the house and explaining. Luckily someone was in but Widget, being thoroughly frightened and confused by now, kept running away. Eventually I managed to catch her and lifted her back onto the fence so that she could get down into our garden without losing too much dignity!

The coal bunker was another favourite and Pippa was the worst offender here. When it rained she would play with any loose coal and then come in with all four white paws covered in soot!

In the Spring a male and female Mallard visited the pond. This caused great excitement amongst the cats. They all rushed round snickering like mad. The ducks took no notice. We threw them a few pieces of bread but since Koi love brown bread the ducks had a pretty rough ride!

One evening all we could see, behind the rockery, was the tip of the long handle of the fishing net waving gently backwards and forwards. Intrigued we walked slowly towards it. Widget again! She had been nosing around in her usual manner and managed to tip the net over herself! She escaped and shot off just before we rescued her.

Chris's notes still punctuate our lives. "The four paw club have been fed and so have the gill and fin federation", and "back garden watered complete - that includes hanging baskets, rockery and Pippa!".

CHAPTER THIRTEEN:

BLESS 'EM ALL!

Cats are tremendous animals to live with. Ok - so there are the odd heart-stopping moments and periods of intense fury but these are more than offset by their sweetness, their gentleness and their hilarious behaviour.

We have even heard of a Persian cat, called Albert, who is petrified of birds! He will run in as soon as one comes into the garden and refuses to venture out again unless he has a human with him.

We once set a video camera up in the lounge for the evening whilst we went out and caught two offenders on candid camera! Bonnie - at those pesky dried flowers again, and Widget - sitting on the coffee table flinging things onto the floor! They play more when they think they are unobserved - rather like humans in a way.

Occasionally a tom cat will still prowl and howl outside. "Perhaps he remembers **that** year!", I laugh. "Well", Chris retorts, "I wish he'd forget!"

We had to weigh Widget on our kitchen scales but she shot off onto the kitchen top and we had to help her down. Then she and Bonnie - who had been showing her usual interest - went out of the cat flap together! They got stuck! Four back legs see-sawed. Eventually Bonnie squeezed out first. Both of them look a little thin for a couple of hours.

Feeding time is fun. They sit by the patio doors in the kitchen, snickering at the birds outside, as one of us prepares their food before taking it through to their room. One day I tore a piece of paper towelling off the holder. Four cats took off as one and fled, in total silence, out of the room. Sometimes they will do this for no apparent reason. Not one that we can see anyway. Very disconcerting.

They all feed differently of course. Phoenix is neat and tidy. Widget yells even when the food is down, Pippa flings hers all over the floor and Bonnie always waits until everyone else has finished. Not surprising really!

Widget and Bonnie both watch TV. Bonnie sits on the back of their chair very quietly, the only movement being her head as it swivels from side to side. Widget sits on the floor underneath the television and suddenly springs at something she sees, tapping the screen madly until the picture changes. If we change channels with the remote control it beeps and she goes berserk since she obviously believes there is a mouse in there somewhere!

Throw a wadded piece of paper at Pippa and she ignores it. Phoenix, however, will immediately run to it, pick it up in his mouth and take off with it, at which point Pippa decides it was meant for her after all!

There they sit - staring at something always beyond your sight, hoping that you will get up to see what on earth is going on and thus be halfway to getting their breakfast or playing a game with them. They lie around like multi coloured scatter cushions.

Be spellbound at the way they delicately lick a paw then pause to watch or listen with paw still raised and curled, sometimes with the tip of a small pink tongue left out.

Touch a cat and feel it sing. Watch their dainty dancing.

PIPPA

is the original farmhouse cat. She could never be called a 'Farm' cat because she is too fat. Many black and white cats do tend to become bulky and the fact that she is long haired doesn't help! She lost quite a bit of weight once the kittens were over a year old and we could exchange the 'growth' biscuits for normal ones.

She is totally scatty. She comes and goes, sometimes snooty, sometimes loving. I wrote the following poem for her because she kneads our white bedroom rug so much. The poem is meant to be sung to the tune of "When the train is in the station" or, more correctly, "Humoresque" by Dvorak.

"I'm a happy little catty, when I'm playing on my mattie
I'm a happy catty yes I am
I can play in front of Mummy 'cos she thinks I'm very funny
I'm a scatty catty yes I am".

The singing seems to make her worse.

Most of her sleeping time is spent flat on her back with legs splayed and much white tummy showing. Very unlady like! Chris leaves 'post-it' notes for her on the back of his chair. "Pippa please do not sleep on this top!"

Pippa sits and thinks - or just sits - a black and white statement at the end of the bed. Sometimes a solitary loud meow will occur before tubby paws are plonked on a human midriff.

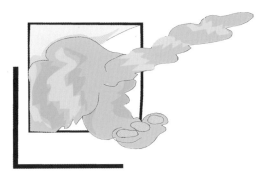

BONNIE

is a ready built shadow. She is often missing because she slinks behind us and gets shut in. There was the famous time she managed to get locked in for the night in our porch and the postman dropped our mail, by mistake, onto her head! Over the years she has managed to get shut in rooms, sheds and garage. The only time she speaks is when she is let out!

She tries to get into the television set if there are birds calling during a programme. She is our 'granny', always fussing us and making sure we are in bed before she will settle for the night and go about her own routine. She emits faint, doll like squeaks if she is picked up!

Bonnie takes messages! Some cats come immediately when you call and others are like her - arriving when you think they've left home.

One evening I left a note for Chris asking him to let me know if he'd seen her before he went to work the following morning. I came down to find not a cat in sight but the following message:

CAT ATTENDANCE SHEET FOR WEDNESDAY 2ND AUGUST 1995

CAT	ARRIVAL TIME
PIP	0638
BON	0643
PHOENIX	0645
WIDG	0648

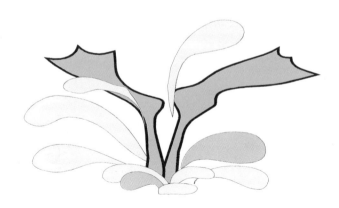

Sleek and satiny with the sweetest of natures, she never misses a trick! I once tried putting a 'post it' note on her head asking Chris for coffee but she soon shook that off and shot up the garden!

Obviously much rough paper has been thrown into bins during the preparation of this book. We have a large paper sack for all our discarded scraps of scribblings. Bonnie insists this is now her bed!

Her eyes shine bright gold from her intelligent jet black face - a homing beacon in the darkness.

Can you see a seagull darling
Floating in the sky?
Or are you merely watching
The clouds as they roll by?

~~~~~~

PHOENIX

is the "Tyger burning bright". When he first visited the Vet they took one look at the size of his paws and said, "he's going to be enormous!" They were right.

Although he very soon learned that his size gives him an unfair advantage and occasionally realises that 'paw is law', nonetheless he has a stable relationship with the family and has grown to be not only good natured but extremely gentle with us all!

He has the most beautiful coat and colouring. He is shy, sensitive, dreadfully unruly and totally loving all at the same time. He likes worms. He also catches quite a few birds unfortunately.

"If he's upstairs", Chris says, "Look out for toads, frogs, gnomes and fairies!"

Phoenix will roll over to show his honey coloured tummy in total sublimation. He almost apologises as he falls halfway downstairs before regaining his regal bearing and swishing his long, long tail with the sheer joy of life.

WIDGET

is courageous and has been from the start - if only to survive. Our garden still remains her kingdom most of the time.

What can you say about an eternal kitten? She will never grow large like her cousin. It took her 6 months before she could get on top of the old scratch post we had which was much shorter than the one we have now!

Pick her up and four legs are immediately placed rigidly against your chest. Invite her onto your lap and she declines but rolls all over the floor in ecstasy because she's been noticed!

She is also the only one who meows. Ear splittingly! The others don't. If they are hungry they have spats with each other and walk silently around us until they are fed. Widget tells everyone when to go to bed - or when there is no food left.

Her colouring speaks volumes. She can be scared, bold, silly and wise all at the same moment. Her little head pops up over the top of the single lounge chair looking for all the world like the all knowing, all seeing, long-eared 'Yoda' in 'The Empire Strikes Back'.

She chats all the time - mostly to herself while she plays - and she remains a loner - a legacy from the time before the Widget Steps.

ADVICE

When meeting a cat for the first time get down on your hands and knees. You are much taller than they are and they tend to take this as a threat. Talk quietly - and don't extend your hand until they've accepted you.

If introducing a new cat to the household where others already live it is always best to keep the newcomer in one room for a few days with the door shut so that the cats can get used to the smell of each other. Alternatively, wipe the cats' coats with a solution of one tablespoon of cider vinegar to two pints of water making sure you don't touch their eyes and mouths or any cuts or scratches. When dry they should accept one another.

Bulk out cat food by using up to one third cooked potato or boiled rice mixed with two thirds of their regular tinned or dry food or fish. For a real treat, spread thinly cut wholemeal bread with marmite or similar. Cut into small squares and be careful not to lose your fingers!

Cats Protection League - Head Office - 17 Kings Road, Horsham, West Sussex, RH13 5PN. Telephone: 01403 221900. Facsimile: 01403 218414. Helpline: 01403 221927.

'Night, 'night!